Bits in the Jam

Copyright © Elisabeth Sherriff 2024

Second edition
First published in 2023

All rights reserved

The characters and events portrayed in this book are fictitious. Any similarity to real persons, living or dead, is coincidental and not intended by the author.

No part of this book may be reproduced, or stored in a retrieval system, or transmitted in any form or by any means, electronic, mechanical, photocopying, recording, or otherwise, without express written permission of the publisher.

ISBN: 978-1-0687259-3-7

Bits in the Jam

and other poems

Elisabeth Sherriff

For all the awesome little people
who have ever struggled
with bits in the jam.

CONTENTS

Where Do You Eat?	9
Mum Says	10
Have You Ever Seen a Candy Floss?	12
Bits in the Jam	16
My Happy Place	18
Don't Let the Peas Touch the Mash	20
Baking Buns	22
Mini Scotsh Eggs	26
Lasagne for Tea	30
Doughnuts	33
Grow Your Own!	34
Christmas Dinner	36
Picnic Haikus	38
Fussy Eater	40
Dinner Time!	42
Going to the Supermarket	46
Eggcellent Eggs	50
Fish and Chips	54
Dad's Doing a Barbecue	58
What Do You Like?	60

Fish Is Too Fishy	64
Ice Cream	68
Picky Lily	69
Fruity, Veggie ABC	70
Gravy Makes Me Wavy	74
Eat a Rainbow	78
My Friend's House	80
Self-care Haikus	84
Relax!	86
A Riddle	88
Even Peas Have Birthdays!	89
An ABC of ME	90
Amazing Me!	92
My Favourite Food	93
Food I Might Try	94
Acknowledgements	96
Books by the Same Author	98

Where Do You Eat?

Some families eat
at the kitchen table

some families eat
on the sofa
in front of the telly

my favourite place is
at the picnic table
in the garden
on a summer's day.

Mum Says

Mum says vegetables are healthy

and fruit is good for me

Mum says one day I'll empty the fridge

and be as tall as the tallest tree

Mum says I'll be a human dustbin

and eat twelve sausages for my tea

Mum says that I am perfect

and that she'll forever love me.

Have You Ever Seen a Candy Floss?

Have you ever seen

a sausage roll

a fig roll

an apple crumble

an apple turn over

a milk shake

a chocolate flake

a Viennese whirl

a candy floss

a hot dog

a chilly chilli

a shy coconut

a bean run

a potato do the mashed potato
a potato in a jacket
a broad bean abroad
or a soldier in an egg?

Have you ever
been to sea in a gravy boat
counted the fingers on a fish
or wrapped a pig in a blanket?

Have you ever
found a toad in a hole?

My favourite breakfast is definitely dippy eggs with toast soldiers. I like my eggs just a little bit runny so I can get a good dunk!

Bits in the Jam

Your turn to make a sandwich, Fred
have you washed your hands?
Mrs Lamb said

yes, Mrs Lamb

put two slices of bread on your plate,
Fred

is it white bread?

yes, Fred

are there any bits in the bread?

no, Fred
it's plain bread

good
said Fred

now spread some butter on your bread, Fred

is it butter?
it looks like spread

oh yes
it's spread, Fred
said Mrs Lamb

I like spread
said Fred

now some jam, Fred

are there bits in the jam, Mrs Lamb?

no, Fred
it's smooth jam
that's it
spread it on your bread
pop the lid on, Fred
you can lick the jam from your hand
said Mrs Lamb

good
said Fred

well done
that's a great sandwich, Fred!

thank you!
I like jam, Mrs Lamb.

Don't Let the Peas Touch the Mash

What's for dinner, Mum?
I asked
sausages, mash and peas
said Mum
can I have ketchup?
I asked
please!
reminded Mum
please
I replied
ok, sweetheart
said Mum
don't let the peas touch the mash!
I said
Mum sighed.

What's for dinner, Mum?

I asked

fish fingers, mash and peas

said Mum

can I have ketchup?

I asked

please!

reminded Mum

please

I replied

ok, sweetheart

said Mum

don't let the peas touch the mash!

I said

Mum sighed.

You can change the words. For example, you might not like broccoli touching your mash or beans touching your chips.

Baking Buns

I like to bake buns

sometimes with Dad

sometimes with Mum

first the flour

tip into the sieve

oops!

some on the counter

and sift

next the butter

scoop into the bowl

oops!

some in my hair

and mix

then the sugar

pour into the bowl

oops!

some in Dad's slipper

and stir

then the eggs

crack into the bowl

oops!

some on the cat

and whisk

spoon into cases

into the oven

oops!

some on the floor

and wait

onto the rack

let them cool

oops!

one in the dog

and ice

onto the plate

onto the table

oops!

one slid off

and eat!

(But not the one that landed

icing-side down in the dog bed!)

Mini Scotch Eggs

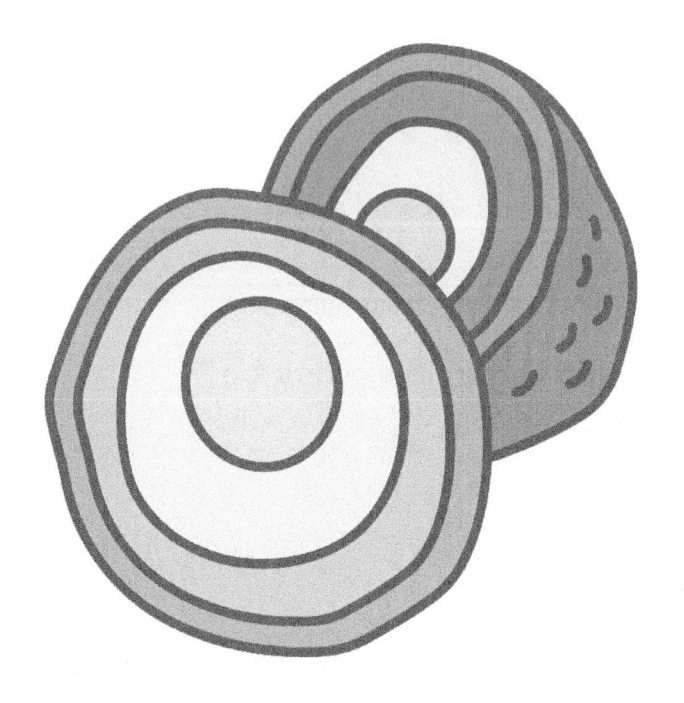

Does your family like mini Scotch eggs?

we all like Scotch eggs

I like mine with pickle

what about Dad?

Dad likes his cut into halves

what about Mum?

Mum likes hers with ketchup

what about Nan?

Nan likes to eat hers with gherkins

what about Gramps?

Gramps likes his with chutney

what about Tom?

Tom eats his straight from the fridge

what about Sophie?

Sophie picks out the middle

have I forgotten anyone?

no... actually, yes!

who?

Smudge

the cat?

yes, the cat

Smudge likes to play football with his!

Lasagne for Tea

Mum made lasagne

for tea

I didn't like it

I got cross

Mum got cross

I cried

Mum cried.

Mum made quiche

for tea

I didn't try it

I got cross

Mum got cross

I cried

Mum cried.

Mum made macaroni cheese

for tea

I tried it

I liked it

I was happy

Mum was happy

I smiled

Mum cried.

Grown-ups worry about what their children eat; they want you to be healthy. Parents can get upset if mealtime goes wrong.

Doughnuts

Fresh-baked
doughnuts

wide grin
big bites
oozing jam
sugary lips
sticky fingers
sugar rush.

Grow Your Own!

Rake the soil

sow the seeds

sprinkle with water

and wait.

Watch the shoots grow

sprinkle with water

pull out the weeds

and wait.

Tie them to sticks

sprinkle with water

hope the sun shines

and wait.

Pick the tomatoes

carefully into a bowl

wash under the tap

and eat.

Christmas Dinner

Some families like

a roast turkey dinner

with pigs in blankets and gravy

some families like

a vegetarian dinner

with piles of yummy vegetables

some families like

a lamb curry

with naan and mango chutney

some families like

fish and chips

with vinegar and mushy peas

my family likes

to make our own pizzas

with our favourite toppings.

Picnic Haikus

Picnic on the beach

sand in our ham sandwiches

no one minds at all.

Sitting by a stream

a dragonfly flutters by

spilt squash on the rug.

Top of the mountain

share hot chocolate from a flask

an amazing view.

Picnic in the car

burgers in soft buns with fries

ketchup on my chin.

Fussy Eater

People say I'm a fussy eater

but Mum says

I just haven't found what I like yet

People say I'm a fussy eater

but Nan says

I'm just choosy

People say I'm a fussy eater

but Gramps says

Mum shouldn't worry

People say I'm a fussy eater

but Dad says

I'll get there one day.

Dinner Time!

Luna has forgotten her lunchbox

and Joah has dropped his juice

what time is it?

dinner time!

Yolanda's yogurt has exploded

and Daisy is under the desk

what time is it?

dinner time!

Connor is covered in custard

and Jemima is sitting on jam

what time is it?

dinner time!

Selina has slipped on a strawberry

and Grant has a grape in his ear

what time is it?

dinner time!

Max has thrown mash at Mia

and Kris has crisps in his shoe

what time is it?

dinner time!

Sam is sitting on a satsuma

and Hattie has ham in her hair

what time is it?

dinner time!

Mrs Cole has dropped the slop bowl

and Pippa has pea'd on the floor

what time is it?

time to ring the bell!

Going to the Supermarket

Mum, what's that aisle?

fruit and veg, Joe

oh, we don't need to go there

oh, yes we do!

Mum, what's that aisle?

juice and squash, Joe

can I have blackcurrant, please?

I should think so

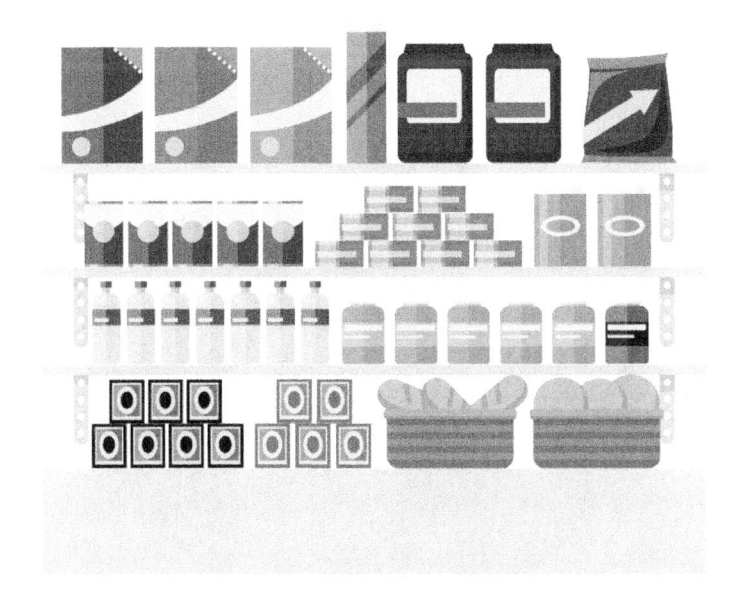

Mum, what's that aisle?

snacks and biscuits, Joe

ooooh, can I have chocolate cookies, please?

if you're good

Mum, what's that aisle?

toiletries, Joe

do they sell toilets?

no, soap and shampoo

Mum, what's that aisle?

babies, Joe

can I have a baby brother, please?

Mum tripped over her trolley wheel.

When you go to the supermarket, perhaps you could choose some new things that you would like to try. You could make a list before or see what looks interesting when you get there.

Eggcellent Eggs

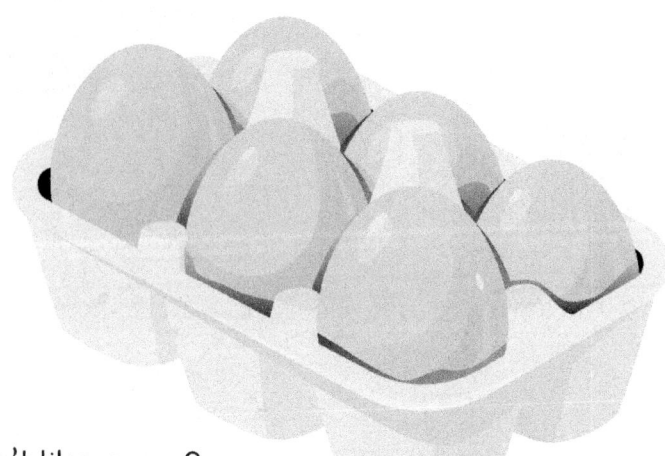

Don't like eggs?
have you tried...

poached eggs
fried eggs
omelette'd eggs
soft boiled eggs with soldiers
hard boiled eggs
baked eggs
sunnyside up eggs
sunnyside down eggs

chicken eggs

duck eggs

ostrich eggs

emu eggs

goose bumps

oops! goose eggs

quail eggs

pigeon eggs

pleasant eggs

oops! pheasant eggs

crocodile eggs

(a snappy snack)

octopus legs

oops! octopus eggs

over-easy eggs

under-easy eggs

(is that a thing?)

mollycoddled eggs

oops! coddled eggs

egg custard

one hundred-year-old eggs

(never in a hundred years!)

pickled eggs

souffle'd eggs

Scotch eggs

Irish eggs

Swedish eggs

or Easter eggs?

phew!

that's more than a few!

I'm sure if you try

you'll find that you do

like eggs!

I have heard that you should try new foods twelve times before you decide if you like it or not. That's eggsactly a dozen eggs!

Fish and Chips

What's for dinner, Mum?

I asked

we're going to the pub

said Mum

will there be fish and chips?

I asked

yes, I've checked

said Mum

are they fat chips or skinny chips?

I asked

both

said Mum

good!

I said.

What's for dinner, Mum?

I asked

we're going to Nan's

said Mum

is she doing fish and chips?

I asked

you know she always does

said Mum

will she do fat chips or skinny chips?

I asked

whatever you like, sweetheart

said Mum

good!

I said.

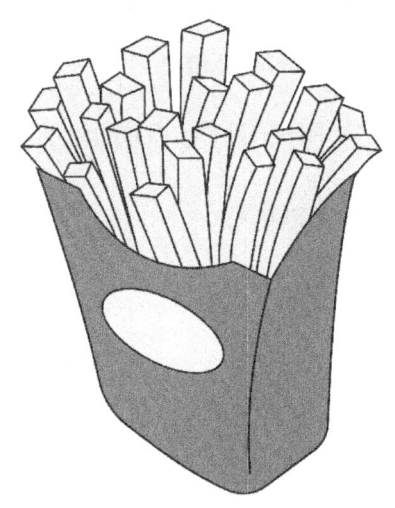

What's for dinner, Mum?

I asked

we're going to the chippy

said Mum

will there be fish and chips?

I asked

what do you think?

said Mum

what if they've run out

I said

I doubt it

said Mum

I think I'd rather have pizza tonight

I said

Mum sighed.

Going out to eat can be quite a challenge if you are not sure what will be on the menu and if you don't know if you are going to like it. Also, it might taste a bit different to the food you have at home. You can always look at the menu online before you go. Don't tell Mum and Dad, but it might taste better than home cooking!

Dad's Doing a Barbecue

Dad's doing a barbecue

I hope it doesn't rain

last time it tipped it down

the weather was insane.

Dad's doing a barbecue,

I hope it doesn't burn

last time he spoilt the meat

maybe Mum should have a turn.

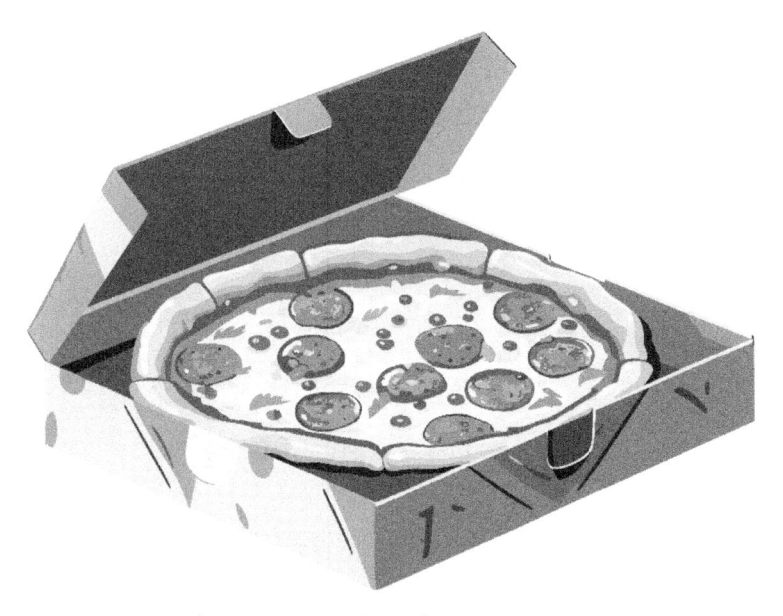

Dad's doing a barbecue

I hope the dog stays in

last time he stole the rolls

we had to get pizza in!

What Do You Like?

Pam likes jam

Ollie likes a lolly

Pete likes meat

Una likes tuna

Mrs Dee likes tea

Mrs Yoffee likes coffee

Rod likes cod

Jake likes cake

Mr Davy likes gravy

Meg likes egg

Peppa likes pepper

Fred likes bread

and Dennis delights

in dunking doughnuts

in Dijon!

We all have our favourite food and drink; mine is probably cheese on toast. We all have food that we are not keen on. I don't like tea; I think it smells bad and tastes revolting. I once tried baby eels. I won't do that again!

Fish Is Too Fishy

My brother thinks that...

eggs are too slimy

carrots are too crunchy

pickled onions are too pickly

pretzels are too salty

oranges are too peely

strawberries are too pippy

sprouts are too sprouty

crisps are too crispy

toffee is too chewy

tapioca is too nobbly

sago is too bobbly

sweetcorn is too bitty

rock is too hard

butter is too buttery

lemonade is too fizzy

fish is too fishy

honey is too runny

and cabbage just stinks

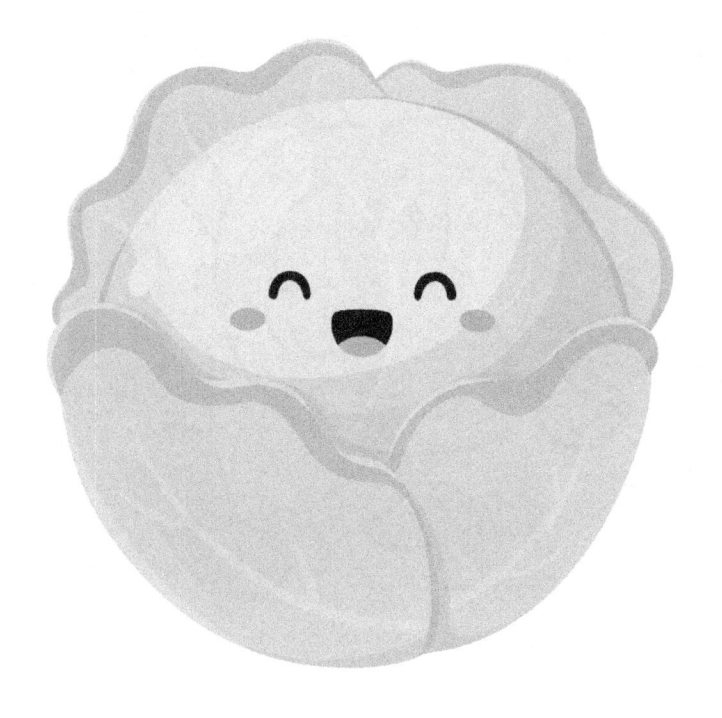

My brother thinks that...

chicken nuggets are great

you can bet

he always cleans his plate!

Some children find the texture, smell or taste of some food unpleasant, but it is always worth trying new food and giving it a chance. Most adults would say that they like some food that they didn't like as a child.

Ice Cream

Swirly whirly ice cream
on a summer's day

lick it fast
before

sticky

sweetness

runs

all over

my fingers

and

trickles

down

my

arm!

Picky Lily

Picky Lily

picked a lily

in Piccadilly

whilst eating

piccalilli.

Fruity, Veggie ABC

Here's my fruity, veggie ABC

lots of tasty treats

for you and for me

why not try some

from the list?

or maybe pick some

that I've missed.

Appetising apricots

Brilliant broccoli

Cool cucumber

Delicious dill

Excellent eggplant

Fabulous fennel

Gorgeous grapes

Healthy haricot

Ideal iceberg

Juicy jackfruit

Colorful kiwi *(I know!)*

Luscious lychees

Marvellous marrow

Nourishing nectarine

Orange oranges

Perfect pineapple

Quality quince

Ravishing radishes

Scrumptious strawberries

Tasty turnips

Unbeatable ugli fruit

Versatile vanilla

Wonderful watercress

eXcellent xigua *(look it up!)*

Yummy yam

Zesty zucchini

There are thousands of different types of fruit and vegetables around the world and quite a few in your local supermarket. I am sure that, if you keep trying new fruit and vegetables, you will find some that you really like.

Gravy Makes Me Wavy

Sometimes food isn't fun because...
pie makes me cry
yolk makes me choke
peas make me wheeze
cheese makes me sneeze

curry makes me worry

mince makes me wince

peel makes me squeal

tea makes me wee

sauce makes me hoarse

mustard makes me flustered

liver makes me quiver

butter makes me splutter

pineapple makes me whine-apple

fruit makes me toot

gravy makes me wavy

and

baked beans

just

make

me

fart!

Sometimes food isn't fun

but there is nothing better

than a plateful of tasty nuggets

and oodles and woodles

of yummy noodles!

Eat a Rainbow

Mum says
I eat too much beige
like chicken nuggets, chips and pasta
and that it's not healthy.

Mum says
I should eat a rainbow
like strawberries, peas and sweetcorn
and that I'll grow tall and strong.

I say to Mum
don't worry
it's ok
I like Skittles!

My Friend's House

My friend Molly invited me

to her house

for tea

I really wanted to go

but what if

they gave me

food I didn't like?

Molly said
we could play
in the garden
but what if
I started
to worry?

Molly said
I could ride
on her new scooter
but what if
I needed
to go home?

Molly said
I could go
to her house
again

I'm glad
I went
but what if
she comes
to my house
next time?

It can be stressful going to other people's homes, especially for the first time. Your friend's family may eat different food and have different habits to yours. Perhaps you could just go for a short visit and your adult could stay while you are there.

Self-care Haikus

Go for a long walk

search for wonderful creatures

paddle in a stream.

Take a bubble bath

share a book with your grown-up

mug of hot chocolate.

Relax!

Lie on your bed
empty your mind
rest your head
relax your spine

heavy as bricks
relax your bum
heavy as trees
relax your tum

breathe in deeply
close your eyes
breathe out slowly
relax your thighs

count to ten

relax your nose

that's too silly

relax your toes

heavy as trucks

breathe in deeply

heavy as moons

hope you're sleepy.

A Riddle

What do you get

if you cross

an expensive car

with a posh chocolate?

A Ferrari Rocher!

Even Peas Have Birthdays!

A
pea
birthday!

An ABC of Me

Being autistic is only part of me

there's one zillion times more

than a whole ABC

I'm

Awesome

Brilliant

Clever

Determined

Entertaining

Fun

Gorgeous

Humorous

Intelligent

Jolly

Knowledgeable

Lovely

Marvellous

Neat

Observant

Proud

Quirky

Remarkable

Skilled

Talented

Unique

Valued

Wonderful

Xcellent

Yummy

Zany

If I had to choose one word

to best describe me

that word is awesome

that's plain to see!

Draw a picture of yourself and add words that describe amazing you.

Draw a picture of your favourite food.

Draw a picture or write a list of some of the things you might like to try one day.

A huge thank-you to my husband for his endless patience and to all the members of Suffolk Writers Group who have advised and encouraged me on my writing journey.

Books by the same author:

Celandine's Gift
Don't Let the Peas Touch the Mash
In My Daydreams
Moon Dust

Printed in Great Britain
by Amazon